George Washington Carver

By Lynea Bowdish

Consultant
Nanci R. Vargus, Ed.D.
Assistant Professor of Literacy
University of Indianapolis, Indianapolis, Indiana

Children's Press®
A Division of Scholastic Inc.
New York   Toronto   London   Auckland   Sydney
Mexico City   New Delhi   Hong Kong
Danbury, Connecticut

Designer: Herman Adler Design
Photo Researcher: Caroline Anderson
The photo on the cover shows George Washington Carver.

Library of Congress Cataloging-in-Publication Data

Bowdish, Lynea.
George Washington Carver / by Lynea Bowdish.
 p. cm. — (Rookie biographies)
Summary: An introduction to the life of the African American scientist who
overcame great hardship to make unusual and important discoveries in the field
of agriculture.
Includes bibliographical references and index.
 ISBN 0-516-23610-5 (lib. bdg.)   0-516-24644-5 (pbk.)
 1. Carver, George Washington, 1864?-1943—Juvenile literature. 2. African
American—agriculturists—Biography—Juvenile literature. 3. Agriculturists—
United States—Biography—Juvenile literature. [1. Carver, George Washington,
1864?-1943. 2. Agriculturists. 3. Scientists. 4. African Americans—Biography.]
I. Title. II. Series: Rookie biography.
 S417.C3B68 2004
 630'.92—dc22

                    2003013683

CHILDREN'S PRESS, and ROOKIE BIOGRAPHIES®, and associated
logos are trademarks and or registered trademarks of Scholastic Library
Publishing. SCHOLASTIC and associated logos are trademarks and or
registered trademarks of Scholastic Inc.
7 8 9 10 R 13 12   62

Peanut butter

Do you know 300 things you
can make from peanuts?

George Washington Carver did.
He was a scientist. He found
new ways to use crops.

He made many things from peanuts, pecans, and sweet potatoes.

Sweet potato

6

Carver was a teacher, too. He helped farmers grow better crops.

He spoke to people around the country. He wanted them to know what they could do with the things they grew.

Carver was born in Missouri around 1864. Carver's mother was a slave.

A slave is a person owned by another person. At that time, people sold slaves to each other.

Soon after Carver was born, slavery ended.

A place where slaves were sold.

Carver grew up on the farm where he was born. It belonged to Moses and Susan Carver.

They taught Carver how to read and write. Carver loved to learn.

An African American school

Carver's college class

Carver left the farm when he was about 11 years old.

He went to a school for black children in another town. He had to work to take care of himself.

After many years, Carver went to college in Iowa.

Carver was good in music and art. He was also very good with plants. So, he went to another college to study farming.

When he finished, Carver became a teacher at the college.

Then, Carver became a teacher
at the Tuskegee Institute
in Alabama.

Cotton

Many farmers in Alabama planted cotton. Cotton used up good things in the soil. Carver taught the farmers how to take care of the soil.

Planting different crops helped
the soil. Farmers planted cotton
one year. The next year, they
planted peanuts or sweet potatoes.

These crops put good things back
in the soil. Changing crops helped
keep the soil healthy.

People gathering peanuts

Tuskegee Institute

Carver wanted to help all farmers. He wrote newsletters and spoke to people.

Some farmers could not visit Tuskegee. Carver sent them a special school on wheels.

Carver was in charge of research at Tuskegee. Research is looking for facts.

A scientist who does research asks questions. Then he or she does experiments (ek-SPER-uh-ments) to find the answers.

Carver doing research

George Washington Carver's lab

Carver worked in a lab. That is where he learned new ways to use peanuts.

He made more than 300 products from peanuts. He made foods, medicines, and paper.

George Washington Carver

32 USA

1998

Carver won many awards for his work. His picture is also on a stamp.

He talked to a committee of the United States Congress. He traveled across the country. People everywhere listened to his ideas.

George Washington Carver and Henry Ford

Carver died in 1943. He was buried at the Tuskegee Institute.

His birthplace is a national monument. People travel there to see where one of the greatest teachers and scientists was born.

Words You Know

cotton

George Washington Carver

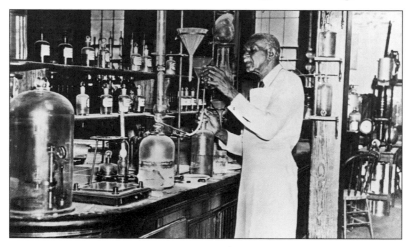

research

national monument

sweet potato

Tuskegee Institute

Index

Alabama, 16–17

Carver, George Washington
  birth, 8
  childhood, 10
  death, 28
  education, 10, 13, 15
  mother, 8
  as teacher, 7, 15–16, 17

Carver, Moses, 10

Carver, Susan, 10

Congress, 27

cotton, 17, 18

experiments, 22

farmers, 7, 17–18, 21

Iowa, 13

lab, 24, 25

Missouri, 8

national monument, 28

peanuts, 3, 5, 18, 25

pecans, 5

research, 22

slavery, 8

soil, 17–18

stamp, 26

sweet potatoes, 5, 18

Tuskegee Institute, 16, 22, 28

About the Author

Lynea Bowdish writes books for children. She lives in Hollywood, Maryland, with her husband, David Roberts, and their dog Princess.

Photo Credits